NIOBE
AND HER CHILDREN

An Inaugural Lecture

BY

R. M. COOK

*Laurence Professor of Classical Archaeology
in the University of Cambridge*

CAMBRIDGE
AT THE UNIVERSITY PRESS
1964

CAMBRIDGE UNIVERSITY PRESS
Cambridge, New York, Melbourne, Madrid, Cape Town,
Singapore, São Paulo, Delhi, Mexico City

Cambridge University Press
The Edinburgh Building, Cambridge CB2 8RU, UK

Published in the United States of America by Cambridge University Press, New York

www.cambridge.org
Information on this title: www.cambridge.org/9781107698468

First published 1964
Re-issued 2013

A catalogue record for this publication is available from the British Library

ISBN 978-1-107-69846-8 Paperback

FOREWORD

This lecture was illustrated by slides. To take their place and for scholarly appearances I have added a catalogue with the usual apparatus. In this tedious work especially I have had the help of many colleagues, to whom I am very grateful. In particular I may mention Professor L. Banti, Mr D. P. Blackman, Mr J. Boardman, Dr D. von Bothmer, Mr M. H. Bräude, Dr B. Conticello, Mrs K. Cook, Professor P. E. Corbett, Dr F. Eckstein, Mr D. E. L. Haynes, Dr R. A. Higgins, Mr J. G. F. Hind, Dr H. Hoffmann, Professor H. Metzger, Frau Professor L. L. Möller, Mr R. V. Nicholls, Dr V. H. Poulsen, Mr M. R. Price, Miss J. M. Reynolds, Dr G. M. A. Richter, Miss J. E. Southan, Dr D. E. Strong, Professor J. M. C. Toynbee, Professor A. D. Trendall, Dr O. W. von Vacano, and Mr A. G. Woodhead.

R. M. C.

The bold figures in the text refer to the list of representations of Niobe and Niobids beginning on p. 41

SIR Perceval Maitland Laurence, who died in 1930, left a generous bequest to the Faculty of Classics. Part of it was used to establish a chair of Classical Archaeology. The first Laurence Professor, appointed in 1931, was A. B. Cook, who had been Reader in Classical Archaeology since 1908. Cook was one of the last polymaths, though his interests concentrated on religion. The three volumes of *Zeus* (two double) are his monument. His successor was A. J. B. Wace, the completest Classical archaeologist this country has produced. His main work was on the Late Bronze Age of Greece itself, and he had the satisfaction of seeing his heresies become orthodoxy. Wace was followed by A. W. Lawrence, a scholar with more conscience and erudition than he liked to admit. He has published standard books on Greek sculpture and architecture, and is now completing a universal history of fortifications. After him came J. M. C. Toynbee, the leading authority on Roman art and one of the few specialists on Roman Britain who understands that 'Roman' has something to do with Rome. She retired only to have more time for study and writing. There is no point in eulogising these four professors; two are now in their prime, and the other two have left works that are very much alive. Instead, I shall mention a predecessor whose merits are being forgotten—Sir Charles Walston (or Waldstein), who came here from America and was Reader in Classical Archaeology from 1883 to 1907 and also, during part of that time, Director of the American School in Athens. Walston was a second-rate scholar, but an organiser of exceptional vigour and imagination. He almost realised the incredible dream of a permanent international corps of archaeologists to excavate Herculaneum, and was baulked only by a patriotic revolt of backbenchers in the Italian Parliament. In Cambridge he was more successful. The creation of this Museum and its facilities for teaching was very largely Walston's doing.

The story of Niobe is old. It was known to Homer, who refers to it casually in the last book of the *Iliad* (XXIV, 602–9). Priam has come to buy back the body of his son Hector, and Achilles has agreed that he shall take it away next morning. So now he invites him to dinner. 'After all,' says Achilles, 'even Niobe did not forget to eat, although she had lost six sons and six daughters in her palace, the sons killed by Apollo with his silver bow and the daughters by Artemis the archeress in anger against Niobe, because she had compared herself with

6

their mother Leto—Leto, she said, had two children, but she herself many. So though there were only two of them they killed all Niobe's children.' A story so moral, and so pathetic too, was very much to the taste of the Greeks and it stayed popular throughout ancient literature. 'What poet has not told of Niobe, mourning her many dead?' as Nemesianus commented in the late third century A.D.—'nam quis non Nioben numeroso funere maestam iam cecinit?'[1] There were, of course, different twists to the tale and even fundamental variations; but the core was normally Niobe's boast to Leto and the shooting of her children by Apollo and Artemis.

The last survey of the subject in art is in Lesky's excellent article in Pauly-Wissowa in 1936, but since then new evidence has turned up and some of the old can be interpreted differently. The earliest known representations are of the 560's B.C., on Tyrrhenian amphoras. Though we must exclude the one Lesky cites, where probably it is Tityos who is being shot, there is no doubt about another amphora bought by Hamburg Museum in 1960 [1]. Here Apollo and Artemis (who curiously is wearing a helmet) shoot at two male and two female Niobids. In publishing this scene Hoffmann argued that, since the gods have only one arrow apiece—on the bow—and their quivers are empty, this must be the version where two Niobids were spared. The interpretation

7

seems to me too clever. If on this pot two of the Niobids were meant to survive, they should be shown escaping behind the avenging gods or protected by some other deity; in Archaic art the action must be emphatically clear. Besides, the Tyrrhenian group, to which this amphora belongs, is a coarsely showy class of Attic Black-figure ware, vigorous in its subjects but very careless in its drawing. So I cannot see any importance in the empty quivers; and even if there were, I should prefer to believe that the gods were each about to kill two Niobids with a single shot.

There are also, as D. von Bothmer tells me, fragments in Leipzig [2] from another Tyrrhenian amphora with the killing of the Niobids. The composition is not certain, but it seems that Apollo and Artemis are both on the left and there are again four Niobids, though one faces the gods while the other three run away.

A good century later, in the 450's, another Athenian vase-painter decorated the well-known calyx-krater[3], which has given him the name of the Niobid painter. Apollo and Artemis and four Niobids are depicted. This is one of the very rare vase-paintings of the second quarter of the fifth century that attempt the new perspective which Polygnotus had just established for painting proper. Depth is indicated by level, but without any diminution of apparent size. So Apollo is meant to be further away than the dead Niobids below him; and indeed he appears to be too, thanks to the rudimentary device of ground lines. Another trick of the new painting is the use of the three-quarter face and the full face instead of the strict profile that was normal in vase-painting.

A sherd in Bonn [4], from a kotyle, is of much the same date. It shows a youth straining with both arms to reach something behind his neck. This is not one of the regular postures of Greek art and needs special explanation. The likeliest is that the youth is trying to pull an arrow out of his back. If so, he may well be a Niobid, though not necessarily; on a pot of this shape there is not room for more than three figures on each side. The three-quarter face again suggests a connection with pictorial painting.

A cup by the Philale painter [5] has on its outside two related scenes, though they are separated by the handles. In one Apollo takes one male and two female Niobids, in the other Artemis two males and one female. The style is the normal style of vase-painting. The date is about 430 B.C.

Two sherds of a krater from Populonia [6] show parts of Apollo and two Niobids; and a fragment of a lid in Athens [6A] preserves two male Niobids and part of a third figure. The date of these works too is around 430 B.C.

From the same period, around 460–430 B.C., there are four reliefs or pedimental sets that illustrate the legend of Niobe and her children.

Two small fragments of terracotta[7], from so-called Melian reliefs, present a man holding up a dying woman. These two reliefs, which were taken from the same mould, never had more than the two figures; the irregular outline is familiar in this class, though more often the background was cut away completely. If they are Niobids—and this is at least likely—the story was already well enough known in art to be intelligible in excerpts. Jacobsthal, who recognised the woman as a Niobid, argued that the male figure is bald and must therefore be a peda-gogue: but he has no beard and his chiton is youth-fully short, and the Actaeon—a young man—of another relief from the same hand has his hair hardly more fully modelled.[2] The date of these pieces is about 450 B.C. They may have been made in Melos, but are certainly not Attic.

The three famous statues of Niobids, one in the Terme Museum and the other two in Copen-hagen[8], must be from a pediment. They are generally accepted as originals, very close in date to the Parthenon, of the late 440's or the 430's. I come back to these statues later.

Two smaller figures also in Copenhagen[9] look like more Niobids from another pedimental set of about the same date. They are said to have turned up in the neighbourhood of Castel Gandolfo, a few miles south-east of Rome.

Next, a pair of reliefs known only at second hand [10]. Pausanias in his description of Phidias's great statue of Zeus at Olympia says of the throne on which the figure sat—'on each of the front legs are put Theban children seized by sphinxes, and below the sphinxes Apollo and Artemis are shooting down the children of Niobe' (v, 11, 2). The usual and reasonable interpretation is that the sphinxes served as the front supports of the arms of the throne, and that the Niobids ran along the two sides of the seat. A few years ago the German excavators found pieces of the moulds for the drapery of the statue, and style and context prove that it must have been made about 430 B.C.[3] It is fairly generally thought that we have copies from the Niobid reliefs, made in Roman times. There are a dozen fragmentary marble slabs, near enough in scale and style (which is that current about 430 B.C.) and representing Apollo and Artemis shooting and Niobids being shot. There is also an incomplete disc [29] in the British Museum, which repeats on a smaller scale most of the types of the slabs and supplements them with others in later styles. The general agreement of these reliefs and their frequency argue strongly for a celebrated prototype, and Phidias's Zeus offers the likeliest model. The arrangement of the figures on the original reliefs cannot, though, be demonstrated. Since the disc is round, its designer had to adjust the composition and was as well inept enough to convert a running woman into a dead one simply by laying her flat. The slabs provide no complete series and anyhow vary the order of the figures that they have. As an extreme instance the fragmentary Artemis from the Isthmus—the only one of these reliefs found or likely to have been found in Greece—shows an unexpected hand on her shoulder. Presumably the figures of the original were loosely spaced and moulds for copyists were taken from them separately. Still, some principles of reconstruction seem to be agreed; on each relief there were a god shooting from one end, five Niobids spread out across, and at the other end a group of a woman tending a dying brother or sister.[4]

A battered limestone relief in Cyrene[11] shows Apollo shooting and a male figure on his knees in front of him; behind Apollo is Artemis (since she wears a short skirt), but she is only urging him on and, if she has a bow, she must be carrying it at the trail. This relief, which comes from an altar, gives the left half of the original decoration, so that we may expect three or four more figures to the right. The subject is usually taken for a massacre of the Niobids; but since Artemis looks like a spectator, what we have might be one of Apollo's single victims (such as Tityos), though one would then have to explain why the god appears to be shooting over his victim's head. The stone is said to be local. The date is not much before 400 B.C.

There are a few other figures of the second half of the fifth and the early fourth century which could be sons and daughters of Niobe, running or hit. Since there are no certain representations for another two generations after them, it is convenient to reflect on what we have so far.

But first, another vase by the Niobid painter, a little earlier than the krater already mentioned[3].[5] This is regularly said to be Artemis and Niobe, trying to save an infant child. The theme would have to have been well known for such an excerpt to be recognisable, and yet infant Niobids appear nowhere else in Greek art. It looks much more like Artemis shooting some woman who has got into trouble, and a likely candidate is Callisto. According to Apollodorus one version of her story was that after she had given birth to Arcas Artemis shot her down.[6] Apollodorus is late, but the killing of Callisto and the reason appear in the *Contest of Homer and Hesiod*[7] in a passage which Aristophanes quoted in 421 B.C. in the *Peace*.[8] Further, the painter Polygnotus, an older contemporary of the Niobid painter, put Callisto among the dead in his picture at Delphi.[9] She also had her grave in Arcadia.[10] Not far from this grave—sixty-two stades by Pausanias's road—was the city of Methydrion, which issued coins displaying on the reverse a naked woman with an arrow in her breast and a baby below her.[11] Another Arcadian city, Orchomenus, has a similar reverse type and on the obverse Artemis shooting.[12] These coins were struck soon after 370 B.C. The dying woman and the child must be Callisto and Arcas, as Imhoof-Blumer first observed. Whether or not the vase shows Callisto, there is even less reason to interpret its woman as Niobe.

Now for some conclusions. First, the story of the Niobids is very rare in vase-painting. Out of some 50,000 known Attic pots and potsherds decorated between 600 and 350 B.C. with divine or human figures none shows Niobe and only six or seven show Niobids. Yet the story was popular in literature and familiar enough to the Athenian public for Aristophanes to joke about it (*Ran.* 911). This is a good warning against crude statistical inferences from art to literature or to tastes in mythology. Scholars tend to forget two very important factors, perhaps the two most important factors in the Greek artist's choice of a subject, apart of course from the existence of the subject. These are the capabilities and conventions of the artist and the shape of the field to be decorated. To take the shape of the field first. It is very roughly true that till the 550's the normal field for decoration on a pot was long and low, and that afterwards it was high and relatively narrow. Since it was also normal for figures to be of about the full height of the field without recession in depth, it follows that the earlier vase-painters preferred extended scenes and the later vase-painters small groups. So there are seventeen certainly identifiable instances of the hunt of the Calydonian boar on Attic Black-figure pots, mostly of the second quarter of the sixth century, but only two certain instances in the whole of Attic Red-figure vase-painting.[13] Yet that subject was not neglected in other forms of art of the time; for instance, it occurs three times on Melian reliefs of the mid fifth century.[14] On the other hand the compact scene of Heracles fighting the lion became popular in Attic vase-painting only with the coming of the relatively narrow panel.[15] But more than a generation earlier, before the end of the seventh century, it was the favourite design for panels on Argive shield straps.[16] I expect that the popularity of Theseus can be explained in much this kind of way, without any resort to Pisistratid policy. So for the killing of the Niobids the normal field of Attic Red-figure vase-painting was not convenient, if the story was to be given its full point. Of the two complete renderings the second [5] has the longer, but unfashionable fields of the outside of a cup, and even so is cramped and rather petty; and the first [3] is abnormal in composition and style. The rarity of Niobids in Black-figure vase-painting before the long low field was abandoned may in turn be explained by the capabilities and conventions of the artists of the time. Their stock of poses was limited and it was difficult to give variety to the fleeing or dying Niobids. Further, these vase-painters liked a continuous composition to have its main feature in the middle and movement from the ends to the middle. Though there are enough exceptions to these rules, the awkward extension of the Niobid scene was no encouragement to represent it. It is not surprising that when Attic vase-painters, Black and Red-figure, wanted a scene of mythological archery, they preferred the less interesting story of Tityos, who was a solitary victim of Apollo and Artemis.

For these reasons the rarity of the Niobe legend in vase-painting has no wider significance, and the three representations in sculpture and the one of the terracotta cut-outs make up quite a respectable total for the mid fifth century. Why the Niobids should have had a modest success just then has of course been considered. As I pointed out, the krater by the so-called Niobid painter [3] imitates the new Polygnotan picture-painting in its style and composition.

It is usually supposed that it imitates it also in subject; and though there is no written record of any such painting, this may well be true. Löwy indeed, with the enthusiasm of the dedicated scholar, went so far as to claim that all—or almost all—Greek and Roman representations of Niobids in every medium of art were based on a lost picture. Yet it scarcely needed a picture to popularise the Niobids as a theme of art. They offered an agreeable variety of poses and the alternation of male and female forms— a convenient change from battles of Greeks and Amazons.

But though there was no set formula, some general conclusions are justifiable. First, Apollo and Artemis must be present in person. Secondly, Niobe herself is not in at the death. This is what one would expect in the sculpture of the fifth century and of the fourth century too—direct treatment and no strong display of emotion. It is all very different from Attic tragedy, where strong emotion is enjoyed and Niobe is a central figure. The glib theory that in any culture art and literature are parallel and similar manifestations makes no useful sense. Nor for that matter do the different branches of art keep in step: in the fifth century Greek sculpture was much stricter than painting in its treatment as well as its choice of subjects.

So it is painting that, for a change from the usual

Classical incident, offers a happier glimpse of Niobe's family before she insulted Leto irrevocably—Λατὼ καὶ Νιόβα μάλα μὲν φίλαι ἦσαν ἕταιραι. The painted marble plaque called 'the Astragalizousae'[12] is widely known, though its subject is often overlooked. The woman sulking in the left background is labelled Leto, Niobe is being pushed along to conciliate her by a girl named Phoebe, and in the foreground two other girls—Aglaie and Hileaira—play knucklebones.[17] Though a work of the first century B.C. or A.D., as the lettering shows, the style is that of the very end of the fifth century. Note that though drapery is shaded, female flesh is not; further the lighting is quite even and background is ignored. Some archaeologists say that this is not a copy, but a pastiche: I cannot see why.

In the fourth century some artists turned to the exploitation of emotion. A Greek vase-painting executed in South Italy in the 310's[13] reflects the new spirit. It is one of those big Apulian compositions that sometimes imitate developments in pictorial painting and sometimes too draw subjects from Attic tragedy (see 14). Here, below a row of inattentive deities, Apollo and Artemis from their chariots destroy the Niobids. But Niobe also is on the stage, and the painter has given her emphasis as the focus of a group. Another figure new to art is the old pedagogue. He probably comes from Attic tragedy of the fifth century, as do the nurse and the defiant and doomed father, Amphion.[18]

Another picture on a marble plaque [15], this time from Pompeii, has something of the style of the late fourth or early third century, though its original may be later. Here Niobe is in her palace, clasping at least one daughter to her bosom, and she dominates the scene. Behind to her right the old nurse examines another, wounded daughter.[19] Lack of space as well as the direction of Niobe's look shows that the avenging gods are off stage.

Very much the same effect appears eventually in sculpture. The Uffizi Niobids [16], which were found together in 1583 near the Lateran in Rome, are copies of a group that was popular in Imperial times, to judge by the number of replicas. The largest component is Niobe herself, trying to protect a young daughter. There are also figures of eight or more other Niobids (in graded sizes) and a pedagogue. The date is uncertain. The elder Pliny, talking of sculpture in Rome, made this remark—'par haesitatio est in templo Apollinis Sosiani, Niobae liberos morientes Scopas an Praxiteles fecerit'—'there is a similar uncertainty over the temple of Apollo of Sosius, whether the dying Niobids are by Scopas or Praxiteles' (*NH* xxxvi, 28). The remark is significant as showing that Pliny could not distinguish between the styles of those two famous sculptors of the fourth century; but it has also been used to date the originals of the Uffizi copies to the fourth century and to reconstruct their history with plausible ingenuity. The problem is complicated further because one of the other copies—the Chiaramonti daughter—has much more deeply cut drapery, and it is not clear which is nearer the original. Still, the dramatic emotion of this sculpture seems to me to have no relevant parallels in the fourth century, and I agree with those who date the originals well down the Hellenistic period. It is a pity that A. W. Lawrence, the most perceptive student of Hellenistic sculpture, has not gone further into this obscure period.

That the Uffizi copies were set up as a group seems certain from their having been found together, and there is no good reason to doubt that their originals too were a group. The style of the various figures is consistent and they were all designed to be viewed only from in front. The first intelligent proposal about their arrangement was made in 1815 or 1816 by the architect Cockerell, when he was visiting Florence on his way home from Greece. Cockerell was a keen and honest observer, who had helped to find and had studied the pediments of Aegina (lost to the British Museum because their agent thought the sale was at Malta and not Zante). So Cockerell restored the Uffizi group as a pediment. His corner figures—local divinities—were added *exempli gratia*, a couple of other figures do not belong, and three of the remainder should be combined with a copy in the Vatican to form two groups—the pedagogue with the smallest son and the largest son with a collapsing daughter. The rise of the ground line to the centre is awkward, but not (I feel) impossible in Hellenistic sculpture. Though a pedimental solution has been rejected generally, I do not see why. Anyhow other solutions look worse. Milchhöfer's tableau vivant would have done very well in the eighteenth century at Caserta, but—so far as I know—is not paralleled in antiquity. Sieveking and Buschor produced a sort of non-architectural pedimental composition standing free with a wall behind it, though Buschor finally returned to a pediment. Admittedly, if the originals belonged to a pediment, they must have been taken down before they could be copied.

All the restorations have one thing in common. Niobe dominates the composition, and Apollo and Artemis are not present visibly. This must be right, for several reasons. First, the upward direction of Niobe's look would make it extremely difficult to place the gods in the composition, especially when one remembers that Niobe, though bending over, is seven foot six high. Secondly, no Apollo or Artemis of suitable size and style has been noticed.

Thirdly, in emotional sculpture like this Niobe herself is the most important actor. (It is interesting to trace the admission of emotional effects into Greek art. The first uninhibited, though not very competent, displays are on some Attic White-ground lekythoi of the end of the fifth century, cheap productions for private use and probably influenced by pictorial painting. A generation or more later, emotion appears on grave reliefs, again catering for private customers. But in civic sculpture unrestrained emotion was not accepted till the Hellenistic period.)

A relief from Atalante in Opuntine Locris[17] is uninformative; but the Hellenistic art of South Italy has left us parts of sets of small terracotta reliefs (to be fixed on—it seems—a rounded surface) and among them are several Niobids and a pedagogue[18-19]. Though the full scheme cannot be reconstructed, this must be the new version.

In Etruria the story of the Niobids has been noted only two or three times. The earliest instance is on a sarcophagus from Toscanella[20], dated not too securely in the third century. Apollo and Artemis are present, though they have wings (like normal Etruscan demons) and are seated (for no obvious reason). Just left of centre is the pedagogue. The woman next to him may be Niobe. The man near the right end with a sword could be her husband Amphion, though he appears to be starting back.

A bronze mirror case from Capena has a group of two women supporting a third. These might, but need not be Niobids.[20]

The other certain Etruscan monument[21] is grander. It is one of three sets of pedimental sculpture of terracotta found at Luni and usually dated in the second quarter of the second century B.C. It is not at all clear which fragments belong to which pediment; but assuming—probably rashly—that the latest reconstruction is more or less right, then in the Niobid group Artemis was in the middle, presumably with Apollo. On the right was an armed figure, with a small child between his legs, and a pedagogue. Other certainties or near certainties are four male Niobids, one on a falling horse. There may also have been a Fury. Whether Niobe or any of her daughters were represented is not known. Although the armed figure may be an inept borrowing from the repertory of battle types—and this would not be surprising in Etruria—he may be intended as Amphion. Nor need the Niobid on horseback be a type borrowed pointlessly; the version may be that where the sons were killed out hunting, and this would be a logical reason for the absence of Niobe and female Niobids.

The hunting version is certain on two wall

paintings from Pompeii[22-3] of the late first century B.C. or the early first century A.D. In the better preserved example Apollo is at the very top on the right; only a foot survives. In the centre is a rustic shrine, with a pair of local divinities below. To the left of the shrine game is being driven into nets and scattered about the field are seven male Niobids, on or off their horses, and various attendants. The ivory door of the temple of Apollo Palatine at Rome, described by Propertius, very likely had a scene of this sort too and of earlier date.[21]

A curious effort of about the same date is painted on a wall in the columbarium of the Villa Doria Pamfili in Rome [24]. It is unskilled both in technique and mythological propriety. On the right Apollo sits on a hill; so this should be the hunting scene. But besides two dead or dying sons we have Niobe sheltering a daughter. The figure running up behind Apollo must be Artemis, though unarmed, if indeed it is anyone in particular. In the left half of the field Heracles is freeing Prometheus. I take it that this scene was painted first and the abbreviated and muddled scene of the Niobids was a fill-in.

Another painting[25], from the Casa dei Dioscuri at Pompeii and very little earlier than the destruction of 79 A.D., shows a pair of tripods with seven male Niobids round one and seven females

24

round the other. Some students have connected this painting with an observation that Pausanias made in the mid second century A.D. At the top of the theatre of Dionysus in Athens he visited a cave, τρίπους δὲ ἔπεστι καὶ τούτῳ. Ἀπόλλων δὲ ἐν αὐτῷ καὶ Ἄρτεμις τοὺς παῖδάς εἰσιν ἀναιροῦντες τοὺς Νιόβης—'there is a tripod above this cave too, and in it [or on it] are Apollo and Artemis killing the children of Niobe' (i, 21, 3). The connection is absurd. The tripods of the painting belong to the architectural fantasies of the Fourth Pompeian style and could not be constructed in three-dimensional reality to stand in the open, or at least nothing like them has ever been found. Further, I feel that if he had been referring to the tripod, Pausanias would have used ἐπί instead of ἐν; but it is not worth reading him through to check this. If, though, these Niobids were on a relief inside the cave, a possible candidate was found in the theatre below [28].

The figures of these Niobids are of traditional types, like so many of the figures of the art of the Roman period. The disc in the British Museum [29] is instructive on such borrowings. Some of its types are of the fifth century, for instance the Apollo, but the pedagogue is Hellenistic. It is a concoction, I suppose, of the second century A.D.—and a stupid one too, since a running Niobid has been toppled over to serve as a dead one. Of about the same date are a couple of statuettes of Artemis and of Niobe sheltering a daughter[31], which were found in a Roman villa in Crete: the Niobe recalls, but varies the Uffizi type[16]. There are Niobids too on Arretine relief ware and on Gallic sigillata[26–7], but the remains are very fragmentary. A relief from Nemi[30], known only from a drawing, is perhaps of the first or second century A.D. At the right (missing) end one must restore Apollo, for balance and to justify the direction of the arrow that is sticking into the youth on the ground. This youth and his brother to the right are Classical enough, but the pedagogue and the more than half-naked Artemis are distinctly later. As on the early Hellenistic sarcophagus[20] she sits to shoot.

An important new treatment of the killing of the Niobids appears on mythological sarcophagi of the 130's A.D., so lucidly studied by J. M. C. Toynbee. In the earlier group[32], the finest specimen of which is in the Lateran, the sons of Niobe are on horseback, but the daughters are present too. Though the combination is logically improbable, it is very effective artistically. This is the progressive Classicism of the time of Hadrian. The crowd includes two pedagogues and a nurse—because of their horses brothers are not available to support or be supported by sisters. At the ends Niobe on the

26

right clasps two daughters and on the left Amphion tries to storm heaven. Apollo and Artemis
have no place in this mêlée, though by an unhappy
afterthought they are shown in miniature on the
lid.

Other, slightly later, sarcophagi[33] bring the
gods into the main scene, with a loss of general
artistic coherence. Nor has the designer adapted his
types completely; one of the victims still thinks that
the gods are up above. Note too how ineffective
Niobe has become. Along the lid we have the next
stage of the story; the dead Niobids lie tumbled on
the ground. This may well be another invention of
the creator of the sarcophagi. Anyhow, no earlier
example is known, and it requires a special shape of
field.

At Panticapaeum or Kerch in the Crimea wooden
sarcophagi were often used in the Roman period.
Some of them[34] had relief figures of terracotta,
plaster or wood, fastened along the sides and ends,
and the commonest types seem to have been Niobids. Up to 1900, when the last general study was
done, at least eight sets of these Niobids had been
reported. They include Niobe and the pedagogue,
but no gods. The figures were affixed separately,
sometimes in an arcade, and there was no continuous
treatment. In one instance the occupant of the
coffin wore a diadem with the impression of a coin

of Vespasian, so that that burial is probably of the late first century A.D. Other contexts are of the second century. By style alone these figures cannot yet be dated closely.

So far as I know, no later Niobids have survived, though the commentary of Lactantius Placidus on Statius (*Theb.* III, 194) offers this note, 'nam hodie quoque Niobe sic pingitur: gremium conferta tot natis, dum unum quemque amplecti manibus affectat'—'Niobe is still painted like this today—with her bosom full of children, while she tries to embrace each one in her arms'. The note is inept in its context and it is not known when it was written originally, nor should I care to say whether the masculine 'unum quemque' is significant. But I shall not be surprised if some time a painting answering this description turns up. It would, dramatically, be Niobe's ultimate triumph.

One conclusion that follows from a survey of the killing of the Niobids is that, though types recur, composition varies greatly. I cannot see any dominant influence of some single model, whether a painting or a sculptural group. Another conclusion, which I have already stated, is that at first Apollo and Artemis are the principal actors and Niobe is absent. The introduction of Niobe and with her of the pedagogue (and other attendants) appears to come in painting during the fourth century B.C., in sculpture not before the third. The gods are now optional. In the Roman period older types of various dates are revived and at least once recreated.

The distribution of the theme of the Niobids in ancient art is worth thinking about. It seems to me that it was well known to Greek and Roman artists and they were ready to use it where they could. I have argued already that the variety of poses which it required made it unsuitable for the Archaic pioneers. Their successors in Classical and later times found this variety attractive and they also appreciated the alternation of male and female anatomy, with a good excuse for swirling and slipping drapery. For sculptors (and vase-painters, whose rules normally were similar) the disadvantage was that to be properly intelligible the theme needed a field that had to be within certain limits of size—that is it must accommodate, say, not less than six or more than twenty figures, with an optimum of twelve to eighteen. So the Niobids are very rare in Attic Red-figure vase-painting, and even rarer on gems[35–6]. They did well for sarcophagi, but not for most architectural friezes. And, as it happened, they fitted very conveniently into pediments—we have the remains of at least four, a remarkably large number for this class of sculpture. It is worth comparing the killing of the Niobids with the battle of Greeks against Amazons, which also offered the contrast of male and female bodies and variation in dress and undress. Although in literature the battle of the Amazons was a much less interesting subject than the death of the Niobids, it could be resolved satisfactorily into duels or be extended indefinitely. So Amazons are frequent not only in vase-painting, but also in the whole range of sculpture from squarish metopes to long friezes. The reason is that the choice of subjects in Greek reliefs (and other forms of art) was made normally for aesthetic qualities and not for literary merit or symbolism, though scholars have tried hard enough to find symbolic relevance. So it seems to me absurd to say, as some do, that the Niobids must have had a funerary significance for the ancients because they appear often on sarcophagi. I have been talking particularly of sculpture and vase-painting. In pictorial painting, from Polygnotus on, depth of field and setting were developed. Here there was a new range of treatments of the Niobid story and I imagine that they were exploited, in ways too that Amazons were not.

What started me on this survey of Niobids was the restoration of the group to which the well known figures in the Terme and Copenhagen belong. They were found separately in 1873, 1886 and 1906 in Rome, apparently fairly near one another to the north of the Via XX Settembre in what used

Fig. 1. Dinsmoor's restoration of Niobid pediment to fit temple of Apollo at Bassae. The light figures are extant.

to be the Gardens of Sallust. Material, style, technique, scale and subject make it reasonably certain that they go together and were intended for a pediment. But there are always some scholars who are unreasonable. In particular, it has been argued that the face of the Terme Niobid is wasted if she was set so high up that it could not be seen.[22] This is true, but the unfinished upper surface of the plinth shows that that must have been above eye-level; and if the plinth was above eye-level, the face must have been even more so. Again, it has been argued and is tacitly accepted by most photographers that the principal view should be more or less oblique, although in sculpture of the mid fifth century the maximum lateral extension gives the plane of viewing—that is, it is at right angles to the direction of the viewer. Well known examples of this rule are the Discobolus and the Artemisium bronze. There is perhaps another argument for this Niobid. In her back is a hole for an arrow. Put an arrow in it, and the position in which it projects above the figure should be some guide to the intended front view. Incidentally, there was an arrow in the Copenhagen youth too.

From time to time students have tried to identify other surviving figures from this pediment. The most notable is Langlotz, though so far he has admitted publicly only to a torso in West Berlin, a head in Bonn and an Apollo which I shall mention later.[23]   For the present I am assuming that we have only three figures from our Niobe pediment.

The most recent and explicit of published restorations of this pediment is Dinsmoor's of 1939 (Fig. 1).[24] Like many others he saw a stylistic connection between these Niobids and the pedimental sculpture of the temple of Zeus at Olympia, looked for a suitable temple in the western Peloponnese, and found that of Apollo at Bassae. Dinsmoor's arguments are ingenious and intelligent, and have had a good deal of acceptance.

This restoration fails, I think, for reasons of composition. The most important position in a pediment is the centre, and it is there that the dominant figure or figures should be. Now at Bassae the size of the pedimental field is known and, since the two surviving daughters could not be shifted further to the sides, there is room for only one figure between them. Dinsmoor has to make this Niobe. But, as I hope I have shown, a fifth-century scene of the death of the Niobids should emphasise Apollo and Artemis and omit Niobe. Secondly, the number of figures looks too few for a reputable pediment. To take other pediments of the mid fifth century, the west pediment of the temple of Zeus at Olympia has twenty-one figures and the east seventeen (counting each team of horses as equivalent to two

Fig. 2

34

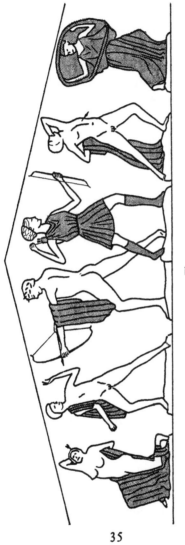

Fig. 3

Figs. 2–3. Hypothetical restorations of centre of Niobid pediment. Only the outermost figures are extant.

35

human units); in each of these pediments the centre is held by a single presiding figure. The west pediment of the Parthenon was even more populous, and it had two central figures, as also had both pediments of the much smaller Nereid monument. The Olympia pediments were carved about 460 B.C., the Parthenon pediments about 435, and the pediments of the Nereid monument about 420. Our Niobids have a formula for eyelids a little more advanced than the metopes of the Parthenon (of the late 440's), but they are unequal in style and it is hard to find close and chronologically useful comparisons. So opinions about their date vary. Some put them within the 440's, others think them retarded (if not provincial) work of the 430's.[25] Anyhow, in a pediment with a scene of action made about this time we should expect at least a dozen figures and should not be surprised if two figures shared the centre. Dinsmoor's table of relations between the sizes of pediments and pedimental figures is, I am afraid, misleading.

It is only fair to Dinsmoor to stick my neck out in turn, and offer another restoration. If the gods are there, they must be in the centre and standing back to back to face their targets.[26] Admittedly the scheme has to be centrifugal; but so too is that of the west pediment of the Parthenon, and there are earlier parallels in vase-painting.

One at least of the gods should be in action. Since the male is conventionally more active than the female, Apollo anyhow must be shooting. Artemis could be either shooting too or taking an arrow from her quiver. For contrast I prefer her taking an arrow. Her skirt could be long or short; but if she is on the right—and I will give a reason for that later—a long skirt would mask Apollo's right leg.

With the gods shooting from the centre, it follows that the Terme Niobid must be on the left and her Copenhagen sister on the right, since those are the directions in which they are trying to escape.

Langlotz has suggested that the missing Apollo is one in the Capitoline Museum.[27] It was found in Rome, near the temple of Apollo Sosianus, a mile and a half from the Gardens of Sallust. Style and action suit well. But the height of this figure, with feet restored, is 1·52 metres—that is only three centimetres more than the Terme Niobid. Since the Niobid's pose is much more contracted, it is obvious that she is on a bigger scale than the Apollo. That by itself seems to me decisive in excluding Langlotz's Apollo from our group; major gods cannot be smaller than human victims, especially if they are young women. Besides the centre of the pediment would be empty at the top.[28]

For the same reason of scale I doubt if the Terme Niobid can be next to the central figures. If straightened out, she would be quite as big as a stand-ing god, even when allowance is made for an out-stretched arm (Fig. 2). Further, the contrast in scale of the Terme and Copenhagen sisters is too obvious if they are in next to central positions; yet because of their heights the two figures must corres-pond. Thirdly, at the scale set by these sisters there would be room in the pediment for no more than ten figures, as Dinsmoor's restoration shows. On the other hand, the scale of the Copenhagen figure would be very diminutive if she was far from the centre. It looks as if the interval between the gods and these Niobids should be either of one figure or possibly of two closely linked figures. Since I sus-pect that the masses of linked figures would attract too much interest to be prudent in a composition already likely to split at the centre, a single figure seems to me more likely (Fig. 3).

For logical and artistic balance these intermediate figures should be male. Further, since the left sister is hit and the right sister not, the right brother should be hit and the left one still unwounded. (Incidentally, the Copenhagen sister is looking not only back, but also slightly downwards, which suggests that what she is looking at is a collapsing figure.) If this restoration is admitted, it is easier to put a shooting deity on the left and a loading deity on the right.

In the left end of the pediment goes the Copenhagen brother, and there is room for two more figures. The pose of the Terme sister leaves a large blank above her right thigh. A figure stooping forward would fit in well and, since the attitude is unmanly, it had better be a female. To fill the last gap something like a wounded youth, sitting on the ground and bending forward towards the corner, would be tolerable. I feel I have done enough without attempting the right corner.

A restoration of this sort is a useful exercise, but it has no validity. One can even work out some sort of odds against its being right, a test of a kind that Classical scholars do not use nearly enough. Let us assume that it is two to one that the gods were in the centre, two to one that their positions and poses were as I have suggested, two to one for the assumption that there was a single figure between the gods and the surviving sisters, and again two to one for the accuracy of the pose of each of the restored Niobids. Then since there are five assumptions, the cumulative odds for the general correctness of Figure 3 as a whole are two thirds to the power of five—or about eight to one against. But some of these odds are optimistic, particularly those for poses, and I should put the chances for the substantial accuracy of my reconstruction as no better than one in thirty. Even so, it seems to me to satisfy reasonable requirements better than Dinsmoor's.

To conclude, the study of the subjects of ancient art is not difficult. But in all problems of interpretation, frequency and restoration the artistic factors must be considered first. After all, Greek and even much Roman art was produced not by scholars, officials or illustrators, but by artists who were working in a tradition that was not hieratic or propagandist but aesthetic.

BIBLIOGRAPHY

K. B. Stark, *Niobe und die Niobiden* (1863). A comprehensive study, now out of date, though his collection of references in ancient literature is still useful.

S. A. Zhebelev, *Materialy po Arkheologii Rossii*, xxiv (1901). Includes a survey of the artistic representations, mainly for transmission of types.

E. Löwy, *Jahrbuch des Deutschen Archäologischen Instituts (JdI)*, 1927, 80–136; 1932, 47–68. A conveniently illustrated attempt to derive most representations of the story, at least typologically, from a lost and unrecorded picture of Polygnotus or his school.

A. Lesky in Pauly–Wissowa–Kroll, *Real-Encyclopädie (RE)*, xvii (1936), 673–706. A comprehensive and judicious survey. (Referred to here as 'Lesky'.)

Many other studies examine part of the material; references to some of them can be found in the list of representations or the endnotes. Generally their wider concern is with the transmission of types.

A LIST OF REPRESENTATIONS OF NIOBE AND NIOBIDS

This list has faults. First, it is not always easy to decide what should or should not be included. Apollo and Artemis have other victims and it is only by the context that they can be recognised as shooting Niobids. A woman, not old, who is sheltering a child is a likely candidate for Niobe. The Niobids by themselves are like other unarmed young men and women in scenes of vigorous or violent action, unless they are being killed by arrows, and even then a single figure is ambiguous. Secondly, I know the majority of the pieces listed only from publications. Thirdly, the dating of many Hellenistic and Roman works is obscure, at least to me.

In citing publications I have noted the principal or most recent studies and the most convenient illustrations. The reader who wants fuller references can work back from those.

I. ARCHAIC AND CLASSICAL ART

Attic Black-figure vase-painting*

1. Hamburg 1960. 1. Tyrrhenian amphora. B. Apollo and Artemis shooting, two youths, two women. By the Castellani painter. 570–560 B.C. H. Hoffmann, *AA* 1960, 77–80, figs. 18-23.

2. Leipzig. Fragments of Tyrrhenian amphora. Apollo and Artemis shooting, three women, one youth. 570–560 B.C.

Attic Red-figure vase-painting†

3. Louvre MNC. 511 (G. 341). Calyx-krater. B, Apollo and Artemis shooting, three youths, one woman. By the Niobid painter. 460–450 B.C. *ARV*, 419–20 no. 20. FR III,

* D. von Bothmer told me of no. 2 and attributed no. 1 to its painter. The scene on the Tyrrhenian amphora, Tarquinia R.C. 1043. (*AD* I, pl. 22; *CVA Tarquinia* II, pl. 1169) has been interpreted as the killing of the Niobids (Lesky, 673; Bothmer, *AJA* 1944, 169, G.1 and cf. G. 6; and now C. Clairmont, *Antike Kunst* 1963, 25); but it makes better sense if the victim is Tityos (J. D. Beazley, *ABV*, 97 no. 32), both because of the cast and because the male fugitive is bearded.

† For the Niobid painter's amphora Paris, Seillère, see p. 13. It is also suggested that there are Niobids on a fragment of a krater of 460–450 B.C. in Rimini, Mus. Missionario (M. Zuffa, *St. Etr.* xxv, Supplement, 'Spina e l'Etruria Padana', 137–8, pl. 18. 6; Clairmont, *op. cit.* 26, pl. 9. 3); but the short skirt and what seems to be a spear make an Amazonomachy more likely. Clairmont also offers the fragment of a cup of c. 430 B.C. in Bologna (G. Pellegrini, *Cat. Vasi Greci Dipinti*, no. 424, fig. 123), on which there appear a wounded naked male and a booted foot; but it would be unusual for a Niobid to have two arrows in him.

pl. 165. T. B. L. Webster, *Der Niobidenmaler*, pl. 2 *b* and 5 *a*. Lesky, 674–5.

4. Bonn 1377. Fragment of kotyle. Part of youth. 470–460 B.C. *CVA Bonn* I, pl. 22. 6. *JdI* 1932, 52, fig. 5.

5. British Museum 67. 5–8. 1066 (E. 81). Cup. *A*, Apollo shooting, two women, one youth. *B*, Artemis shooting, one woman, two youths. By the Phiale painter. *c.* 430 B.C. *ARV*, 659, no. 112. *JdI* 1927, 108, fig. 20 (*A*); 1932, 53, fig. 7 (*B*).

6. Florence, Mus. Arch. Etr.; from Populonia. Fragments of krater. Parts of Apollo shooting and two youths. 440–430 B.C. *JdI* 1932, 49, fig. 1, and 52, fig. 3. *NSc*, 1908, 227, figs. 35–35 *a*.

6 A. Athens, Agora P. 6845. Fragment of lid of pyxis. Two youths and part of a third figure (perhaps five figures are lost). *c.* 430 B.C. *Antike Kunst* 1963, 23–5, pl. 8. 1–2.

Classical Sculpture, etc.

7. (*a*) Berlin, Terr. inv. 6286; (*b*) Oxford 1938. 911. Fragments of two Melian reliefs from same mould. Youth supporting woman. *c.* 450 B.C. P. Jacobsthal, *JHS* 1939, 68–70, pl. 8; *Die Melischen Reliefs*, 62–3, 165–6, pl. 42. (On dating see R. A. Higgins, *Cat. Terracottas in B.M.* I, 165; J. W. Graham, *AJA* 1958, 318.)

8. (*a*) Rome, Mus. Naz. 72274; (*b*) and (*c*) Copenhagen, Ny Carlsberg 520 (Cat. 398) and 472 (Cat. 399). From a pediment. Dying woman; running woman; youth lying on side. *c.* 430 B.C. Br.Br., pls. 706–14. E. Paribeni, *Sc. gr. del V sec.* no. 4 for (*a*). G. Lippold, *Gr. Plastik*, pl. 65. 1–3. G. M. A. Richter, *Sc. and Sc.*², figs. 4, 92, 118. Some other references are given in endnotes 22–5.

9. Copenhagen, Ny Carlsberg 1682 (Cat. 304) and 2749 (Cat. 399 *a*). From a pediment. Running woman; wounded youth. *c.* 430 B.C. Br.Br., pls. 663 and 771. The related pieces Copenhagen, Ny Carlsberg 2222 (Cat. 107) and Berlin K. 7

do not belong to any normal Niobid ensemble and should not be from the same pediment.

10. Copies of reliefs from throne of Phidias's cult statue of Zeus at Olympia. Style of *c.* 430 B.C. (To identify the figures I use the numbering of J. Sieveking and E. Buschor, *MüJb* 1912, 142: nos. *1, 2, 7, 9, 10, 13* are male Niobids, nos. *8, 12, 14* female. *A* is the group of woman and youth, *B* the group of two women.) Lesky, 682–3, 684–7. E. Buschor, *SB Bay. Ak. Wiss.* 1938. 3. O. Waldhauer, *Trudy Otdela Antichnogo Mira* 1, 5–29. W.-H. Schuchhardt, *MdI* 1948, 95–137. G. Becatti, *Problemi Fidiaci*, 135–8, 235–6. W. Fuchs, *Die Vorbilder der neuatt. Reliefs*, 131–2. G. Hafner, *Ein Apollon-Kopf in Frankfurt*, 33–6. C. Clairmont, *Antike Kunst* 1963, 23–32.

(1) Leningrad 352 (K. 337). *A, 2, 1, B; 12, 13, 14.* Waldhauer, *RM* 1929, 199–200, pls. 47–52. Becatti, *op. cit.* figs. 232–5. *JdI* 1927, 101 fig. 18. *JdI* 1932, 152 fig. 1, 156 figs. 4–5. E. Langlotz, *Antike* IV, 31–41, pls. 1, 3, 4.

(2) Rome, Villa Albani 885. *2, 1, Artemis. JdI* 1932, 158, fig. 9. Langlotz, *op. cit.* fig. 3. Becatti, *op. cit.* fig. 236.

(3) Rome, Palazzo Colonna. *1. EA* no. 1161.

(4) ? Vatican (once Kircher). *1. Ber. Sächs. Ges. Leipzig* 1877, pl. 2.

(5) Catania. *7. EA* no. 762.

(6) Bologna, Palazzo Bevilacqua ('Zambeccari relief'). *7, 10. JdI* 1932, 161 fig. 12. Langlotz, *op. cit.* pl. 2. Becatti, *op. cit.* fig. 230.

(7) Florence, Milani collection. *8, 7. JdI* 1932, 160, fig. 11. *JdI* 1927, 100, fig. 17. Langlotz, *op. cit.* pl. 2. Becatti, *op. cit.* fig. 229.

(8) Once Rome, Ludovisi collection. *13. Ber. Sächs. Ges. Leipzig* 1877, pl. 3.

(9) Kassel Sk. 112 (once Klugmann). *Apollo.* E. Berger, *Antike Kunstwerke*, 40–1, fig. on p. 8. *JdI* 1932, 170 fig. 17. *MdI* 1948, pl. 44.

(10) Pozzuoli 104. *A, 2. Boll. di Storia dell'Arte* 1953, 3–4. *Antike Kunst* 1963, 26–7, pl. 8. *3.*

(11) Corinth (from Isthmia). *Artemis*, forearm of another figure (the hand rests on Artemis's shoulder). *Hesp.* 1953, pl. 58 *f*; 1955, pl. 50 *b*. F. Eckstein, *DLZ* 1959, 691. Other fragments found with this piece do not belong to the Niobid series.

(12) British Museum 1962. 8–24. 2 (from Holland House). *14.* C. C. Vermeule, *AJA* 1955, 139. The figure is detached, but the tooling on the edges and the back looks modern.

There have been many attempts at reconstructing the original reliefs, but the possibilities are so many and the criteria so subjective that there is not much purpose discussing them. One of the latest, that of Hafner, segregates the sexes, putting on one relief Apollo, all the male Niobids and his Chloris (see endnote 4) and on the other relief Artemis and the other females: he argues that the literary tradition has Niobe's sons killed by Apollo and her daughters by Artemis, and that in spite even of the Phiale painter's cup [5] there is no proof that artists differed. This is slippery reasoning; which god killed which Niobid was not an organic part of the story, and one of the attractions of the subject for artists was pretty evidently the juxtaposition of male and female bodies.

For the disc in the British Museum, which repeats many of these figures on a smaller scale but adds some later types, see no. **29**.

11. Cyrene 15006. Fragment of limestone altar, probably left part of a sidepiece. Artemis pointing, Apollo shooting, male figure on knees,.... Perhaps *c.* 400 B.C. E. Paribeni, *Cat. Sc. Cirene*, no. 48, pl. 48. *JdI* 1932, 49, fig. 2.

Among other fragmentary figures that may be Niobids I mention these, without any conviction.

(*a*) Copenhagen, Ny Carlsberg 1688 (Cat. 400: the 'Alba youth'). Youth on knees. From a pediment. Early fourth century B.C. Br.Br., pl. 649.

(*b*) Bonn, private collection. Perhaps from a pediment. Male torso. Early fourth century B.C. K. Schefold, *Meisterwerke*, no. 311, fig. on p. 242.

(*c*) Munich 270 ('Ilioneus'). Perhaps from a pediment.

Youth on knees. Perhaps early fourth century B.C. Br.Br., pl. 432.

(d) Frankfurt, Liebighaus. Fragment of relief. Upper part of youth. Date not clear from Reinach's sketch. S. Reinach, *Rép. de la Statuaire*, IV, 368. 10.

Classical Painting

12. Naples; from Herculaneum. Painted marble plaque. In background Leto, Niobe, Phoebe; in foreground Aglaie and Hileaira, playing knucklebones. Signed by Alexander of Athens. First century B.C. or A.D., in style of end of fifth century B.C. C. Robert, *21 Hall. WPr.* A. Rumpf, *MuZ* 122–3, pl. 39. 6. Lesky, 677.

II. HELLENISTIC AND ROMAN ART
(including perhaps some very late Classical)

South Italian Red-figure vase-painting*

13. Ruvo, Jatta 424. Volute-krater. *B*, body: top row—gods, lower two rows—Apollo and Artemis shooting from chariots, Niobe trying to shelter two daughters, pedagogue with son, four more sons and one daughter. Apulian: Baltimore group (late Darian). 320–310 B.C. *Bull. Nap.* I, pl. 3. *JdI* 1932, 60–1, figs. 12–14. Lesky, 675–6.

14. Naples 3246. Amphora. *A*, woman in aedicula, gods, king, old woman, attendants. Apulian: Darius group. 330–320 B.C. *Ber. Sächs. Ges. Leipzig* 1875, 218–29, pl. 4. Lesky, 676–7. Presumably Niobe at the tomb of her children, as in Aeschylus's *Niobe*.

Hellenistic painting

15. Naples; from Pompeii (VII, 15, 2: same house as for no. 22). Painted marble plaque. Niobe sheltering daughter and nurse with another daughter, in architectural setting. First

* I am indebted to A. D. Trendall for dates and attributions.

century B.C. or A.D., in style of late fourth or early third century B.C. C. Robert, *24 Hall. WPr.* A. Rumpf, *MuZ*, 157. C. M. Dawson, *Yale Classical Studies*, IX, 22–3 (he thinks the figures possibly early Hellenistic, but the architecture later).

Hellenistic sculpture, etc.

16. Florence, Uffizi 289 ff., etc. Niobe sheltering daughter, pedagogue with son, son with daughter, four other sons (or five, if the 'Narcissus' is included), two other daughters. Copies of Hellenistic originals perhaps of late third or early second century B.C. G. A. Mansuelli, *Galleria degli Uffizi: le Sculture*, I, 101–21, pls. 70–81.* M. Bieber, *The Sculpture of the Hellenistic Age*, 74–6, figs. 253–65. H. Weber, *JdI* 1960, 112–32. Lesky, 695–703.

Cockerell's pedimental grouping is reproduced by Mansuelli (fig. on p. 101), and the arrangements of Sieveking and Buschor and of Milchhöfer by Bieber (figs. 262–3). Among the few recent students who have pronounced for a pediment are E. Pfuhl (*JdI* 1925, 16–21) and—changing his mind—Buschor (*Plastik der Griechen*, 96).

The Subiaco youth might be a Niobid from another composition. Its original was perhaps of the late third century B.C. Br.Br., pl. 249. R. Carpenter, *MAAR*, XVIII, 25–8, pls. 9–11. G. Lippold, *Gr. Plastik*, 347, pl. 121. 3. Bieber, *op. cit.* 76, fig. 266.

17. Athens, Nat. Mus. 7563. Bronze cut-out relief from Atalante. Woman supported by a larger figure, of which only the right arm remains. Hellenistic. *BCH* 1880, 192–3, pl. 2. A. de Ridder, *Cat. Bronzes Soc. Archéol.* no. 920, pl. 5. S. Papaspiridi, *Guide du Mus. Nat.* 184. Lesky, 690.

* To the replicas cited by Mansuelli add a fragmentary reduced Niobe in Chiusi, Piazza Vittorio Veneto (*JdI* 1960, 118, figs. 6–9); and subtract the bronze head in Berne (K. Schefold, *Phoebus* 1946, 49–59), which is a cast of a modern head (F. Hiller, *JdI* 1960, 133).

18. Vienna. Terracotta figurines in partial relief; from Gnathia. Pedagogue, pedagogue with youth, six other youths, five women: several of the youths have boots and cloaks, so that they are probably hunting. Late fourth or third century B.C. S. A. Zhebelev, *Materialy po Arkheologii Rossii*, XXIV, figs. 52–67. R. Pagenstecher, *SB Heidelberger Ak.* 1910. 6, figs. 1–14. K. Masner, *Die Sammlung ant. Vasen*, nos. 860–73 (other figures, including Artemis, nos. 874–7, probably do not belong to this set). Lesky, 691. Though the backs are curved, some at least of these pieces have holes for nails or pegs, so that it is unlikely that (as Pagenstecher suggests) they were fixed to pots of Canosa ware.

19. Hamburg, Reimer collection. Two similar figurines of naked and barefooted youths; from Canosa. Pagenstecher, *op. cit.* pls. 1–2 a. Lesky, 691.

There are of course other figures that may be Niobids. I mention some that I have noted in publications.

(*a*) Vatican. Similar figurine of youth. W. Helbig and W. Amelung, *Rom*[3], no. 1801 *a*. Lesky, 691.

(*b*) Once in Waddington collection. Terracotta figurine of fleeing youth; presumably from Myrina. Hellenistic. W. Froehner, *Terres Cuites d'Asie Mineure*, 53, pl. 27.

(*c*) Heidelberg 26/56. Fragment of frieze of limestone aedicula; presumably from Tarentum. Woman supporting woman, and a third figure. Later fourth century B.C. H. Klumbach, *Tarentiner Grabkunst*, 12 no. 46, 60-2, 76, pl. 10.

(*d*) Taranto 473/1491. End of pediment of limestone aedicula. Woman lying, woman leaning. Later fourth century B.C. Klumbach, *op. cit.* 2 no. 7, 60-2, pl. 1.

Klumbach thinks it probable that his nos. 48 and 123 also represent Niobids, and concludes that the subject was popular in the minor arts of Tarentum but not of Greece itself.

Etruscan Hellenistic sculpture

20. Vatican, Mus. Greg. Etr. Tufa sarcophagus from Toscanella. Winged Artemis sitting and shooting, youth supporting youth, woman, pedagogue, woman, falling youth, youth, armed beardless male, winged Apollo sitting and shooting. Third century B.C. (so Herbig, without reasons). R. Herbig, *Die jüngeretr. Steinsark.* 44–5 no. 80, 123, pl. 30a. Lesky, 689–90.

21. Florence, Mus. Arch. Etr. Terracotta pedimental figures from Luni. Perhaps parts of Artemis shooting, pedagogue, male with shield, small boy, male on falling horse, three other males,★ and one female (perhaps a Fury): though, as Banti tells me, it is unsafe to rely on the present reconstitution of figures from fragments as well as on their distribution between pediments, yet most of the pieces I have mentioned appear inappropriate to the (supposed) subjects of the other two pediments. Probably second quarter of the second century B.C., for historical and stylistic reasons (though E. M. Richardson, *MAAR* XXVI, 307–8, prefers the early first century B.C.). L. Banti, *Luni*, 49–52, pls. 18–22. A. Andren, *AIRRS* VI, 282, 285, 287–94, pls. 95–6. L. A. Milani, *Mus. It.* I, 89–112, pls. 3–6.

Roman painting

22. Naples; from Pompeii (VII, 15, 2: same house as for no. **15**). Wall painting: top missing. Apollo shooting seven male Niobids, who are hunting round a rustic shrine, attendants, local divinities. Third Pompeian style. End of first century B.C. or beginning of first century A.D. C. M. Dawson, *Yale Classical Studies*, IX, 92 no. 27, 131, pl. 10. H.Br., pl. 151.

23. Pompeii Mus.; from Pompeii (VII, 6(1), 28). Wall painting: only bottom preserved. Part of similar scene, though composed differently (Niobids, attendants, local divinities survive). Third Pompeian style. End of first century B.C. or beginning of first century A.D. Dawson, *op. cit.* 92–3 no. 28, 131, pl. 10. H.Br., 208, fig. 60.

★ Including the male of different clay and poorer style, which with Banti I take to be a replacement for this pediment and not the sole survivor of a fourth pediment.

24. Rome, Villa Doria Pamfili, columbarium (wall B, xx). Wall painting. Niobe sheltering daughter, son fleeing and hit, dead son, Apollo sitting on hill and shooting, Artemis(?) running up. End of first century B.C. or beginning of first century A.D. G. Bendinelli, *Le Pitture del Columbario di Villa Pamfili*, 12, pl. 4. 2. E. Samter, *RM* 1893, 116, fig. 2. W. Binsfeld, *Grylloi*, 34.

25. Naples 1154: from Pompeii, Casa dei Dioscuri. Wall painting. Two tripods, one with seven male Niobids on and round it, the other with seven females. Fourth Pompeian style. Third quarter of first century A.D. L. Richardson, *MAAR* XXIII, 55, 158–9 (by his Perseus painter). H.Br., 180–1, figs. 51–2, pl. 131. Lesky, 680–1, 683–4.

Roman sculpture, etc.*

26. Arretine relief ware: Heidelberg, New York, Munich, Greifswald. (*a*) Woman on knee; (*b*) two women in architectural setting; (*c*) fleeing youth; (*d*) youth supporting woman. Workshop of Annius. Late first century B.C. H. Dragendorff and C. Watzinger, *Arret. Reliefker.* 149–50. R. Pagenstecher, *SB Heidelberger Ak.* 1910. 6, 29–31, pl. 2*b*. Dragendorff, *SB Heidelberger Ak.* 1935–6. 2, 3–9, pl. 1. 1 and 4–6. Lesky, 690. This is the only strictly mythological cycle known from Annius's workshop.

27. Roanne. Fragment of sigillata ware. Boy on knee (probably a Niobid). Probably Central Gaulish. Probably second century A.D. Pagenstecher, *op. cit.* 23 n. 43, fig. 15.

28. Athens, Nat. Mus. mag. 683. Cut-out relief from theatre of Dionysus, Athens. Upper part of youth, stretching back. Larger scale than the figures of the copies of the reliefs from the throne of Zeus [no. **10**] and, though near, not of a type known in their repertory. Probably first or second century A.D. Buschor in FR III, 283–4, fig. 130.

* For much of the dating in this section I am obliged to J. M. C. Toynbee.

29. British Museum 77. 2–27. 1 (Cat. 2200). Marble disc. *Artemis, Apollo; son with daughter, 9, 2, 7, –; 1, 12 and 6, Niobe(?), 14, daughter, daughter; pedagogue and son, 13* (for the numbering see under no. **10**). Second century A.D., in eclectic style. E. Langlotz, *Antike*, IV, 31–41, figs. 1–2, 4–5, pls. 1–2. *JdI* 1927, Beil. 9. *JdI* 1932, 153 fig. 2, 158 fig. 8, 159 fig. 10. *MdI* 1948, pls. 41–4. G. Becatti, *Problemi Fidiaci*, fig. 231.

30. ? Rome, Palazzo Orsini; from temple of Diana Nemorensis, Nemi. Left part of relief. Artemis (half-naked) sitting and shooting, pedagogue with dying youth, youth protesting,.... Presumably first or second century A.D. H. Heydemann, *Ber. Sächs. Ges. Leipzig* 1877, 97–103, pl. 4. 2.

31. Heraklion; from Tsountsouros (Inatos). Statuettes of Artemis shooting and Niobe sheltering a wounded daughter. Perhaps second century A.D. S. N. Marinatos, *AE* 1934–5, 1–17, pls. 1–2. *JdI* 1960, 120–1, figs. 4–5. *JdI* 1932, 56–9, figs. 9–11. In spite of differences it is easier to believe that the statuettes belong to a set.

32. Sarcophagi of Robert's Class II. On sarcophagus: Niobids (males riding), Niobe, Amphion, pedagogues, nurse; on lid: Apollo and Artemis shooting. J. M. C. Toynbee, *The Hadrianic School*, 164, 171–2, 174–5, 184–9. C. Robert, *Die antiken Sarkophag-Reliefs*, III, 373–85.

(1) Rome, Lateran XII, 813. *c.* A.D. 135. Robert, *op. cit.* no. 315, pl. 100. Toynbee, *op. cit.* pl. 37. 2.

(2) Venice. A.D. 140–50. Robert, *op. cit.* no. 316, pl. 100. Toynbee, *op. cit.* pl. 38. 3.

(3) Wilton House. *c.* A.D. 180. Robert, *op. cit.* no. 317, pls. 101–2.

(4) Rome, Villa Giustiniani-Massimo. Fragment. Robert, *op. cit.* no. 318, pl. 102.

(5) Rome, Palazzo Rondinini. Fragments. Robert, *op. cit.* no. 319, pl. 102.

(6) Vatican, Mus. Chiaramonti. Fragment. Robert, *op. cit.* no. 320, pl. 102.

(7) Once Rokeby Hall. Dubious. Robert, *op. cit.* no. 321.

33. Sarcophagi of Robert's Class I. On sarcophagus: Apollo and Artemis shooting, Niobids, Niobe, pedagogue, nurse. On lid: the Niobids lying dead. References as for no. **32.**

(1) Munich 345. *c.* A.D. 160. Robert, *op. cit.* no. 312, pl. 99. Toynbee, *op. cit.* pl. 39. 1.

(2) Vatican, Gall. dei Candelabri. A.D. 160-70. Robert, *op. cit.* no. 313, figs. on pp. 379-80, pl. 99. Toynbee, *op. cit.* pl. 38. 4.

(3) London, Soane Mus. Fragment. Robert, *op. cit.* no. 314, pl. 99.

34. Leningrad; also Odessa, Moscow, Louvre, Berlin. From Kerch (Panticapaeum). Cut-out reliefs of terracotta, plaster or wood, once fixed on the sides of wooden sarcophagi. Groups of Niobe with daughter, pedagogue with son, son with son, daughter with son, son with daughter, and various single figures of sons and daughters and perhaps of pedagogues and nurse. Zhebelev distinguished twenty-five types, though generally the figures of any one type are from different moulds,* and the wooden reliefs give two more types. There are no figures of Apollo or Artemis, nor of fallen Niobids. Apparently the types were used as more or less independent units of decoration; indeed on (7) Niobids were mixed with miscellaneous subjects. Some of these figures were found in contexts of the late first and second centuries A.D., and there is no evidence that any are much earlier or later. The fullest publication, which illustrates twenty-seven examples, is by S. A. Zhebelev, *Materialy po Arkheologii Rossii*, xxiv (1901). I know of these sets.

(1) Found in 1832, on Mount Mithradates (Zhebelev, series I). Plaster. *Antiq. du Bosph. Cimm.* 115, pl. 67. 4-6. *OIAK* (=*CR*) 1868, 58-62, pl. 2. 1-3. C. Watzinger, *Gr. Holzsark.* 58 no. 42, 89.

* There are instances where the same mould was used for figures of terracotta and of plaster (S. Berzina, *Arkheol. i Ist. Bospora*, II, 247-8: this reference and those to Ivanova I owe to J. G. F. Hind).

(2) From same find as (1), but perhaps from another sarcophagus. Terracotta. *OIAK* 1868, 59.

(3) Found in 1862, at the Golden Kurgan (Zhebelev, series II). Terracotta. *OIAK* 1863, 164–72, pls. 3–4; 1868, 62–3.

(4) Found in 1867, on Mount Mithradates (Zhebelev, series III). Terracotta. *OIAK* 1868, 59, 64–5, pl. 2. 4–9; 1867, 11. Watzinger, *op. cit.* 59 no. 53, 89. Same moulds as (3). Found with coin of a Sauromates.

(5) Found in 1874, on Mount Mithradates (Zhebelev, series IV). Plaster. *OIAK* 1875, 6–15, vignette on title-page, fig. on p. 5, pl. 1. 1–3. Watzinger, *op. cit.* 54–5 no. 35, 89, figs. 116–17. Impression of coin of Vespasian on wreath of corpse.

(6) Found in 1891, near road to Khadjimuskai (Zhebelev, series V). Terracotta. *OIAK* 1891, 32–3. Watzinger, *op. cit.* 89 n. 5. Many forgeries were made from moulds taken from these figures and have circulated widely.

(7) Found in 1900. Wood. Watzinger, *op. cit.* 51–3 no. 33, 89, fig. 108 (wrongly described as plaster). A. P. Ivanova, *Antichnya Goroda Severnogo Prichernomorya*, I, 420, fig. 20; *Trudy Otdela Antichnogo Mira*, I, 169, pl. 6. 1. Perhaps found with a coin of Sauromates I (A.D. 93–123).

(8) Found before 1888. Plaster. E. Pottier, *Nécr. de Myrina*, 426 n. 6.

Gems

35. Once Demidoff. Oval. Black agate. Woman protecting youth. Italian Hellenistic (so Furtwängler). A. Furtwängler, *Ant. Gemmen*, pl. 34. 36. Perhaps Niobids.

36. Many replicas. Oval. Glass paste. Woman supporting youth (as group *A* of **10**). Late first century B.C. or early first century A.D. Furtwängler, *op. cit.* pl. 37. 43.

A chalcedony cameo in Vienna with a woman fleeing need not be a Niobid (J. Arneth, *Ant. Cameen*, pl. 17. 8; F. Eichler and E. Kris, *Die Kameen*, no. 58, pl. 11).

NOTES

1 *Cyn.* 15–16, admittedly a rhetorical catalogue of mythological themes. But see the references in Lesky, 645–68: we owe many of them to the trivial curiosity of Aulus Gellius and Aelian about the number of Niobe's children.

2 P. Jacobsthal, *Die Melischen Reliefs*, 31–2, pls. 13–14.

3 *Neue deutsche Ausgrabungen im Mittelmeergebiet und im vorderen Orient*, 277–95, figs. 15–34.

4 E. Langlotz identified as Niobe the woman who holds up a youth (*Phidiasprobleme*, 45). G. Hafner, more logically, makes this woman Chloris, a Niobid whom some authors spared, and sees Niobe in the standing woman of the other group. But the figures have no special characteristics that support such identifications; in a frieze divided into two separate and equal parts Chloris is not a sufficient counterweight to Niobe, and still less is any of her doomed daughters; nor is the sparing of a single Niobid by any means a standard incident.

5 Paris, Baron Ernest Seillère. Amphora. *A*, Artemis shooting, woman carrying baby and fleeing. *c.* 460 B.C. *ARV* 421 no. 40. T. B. L. Webster, *Der Niobidenmaler*, pl. 8 *a*. *JdI* 1932, 64 fig. 15. FR III, 284 fig. 131.

6 III, 101.

7 *Certamen* 9, 17–18.

8 *Pax* 1282–3, quoting *Certamen* 9, 7–8: see A. Busse, *RhMus* LXIV, 114–18, though I do not accept his conclusion that this passage of the *Certamen* must have then been very new.

9 Paus. X, 31, 10.

10 Paus. VIII, 35, 8.

11 F. Imhoof-Blumer, *Monn. Gr.* 200–1, pl. E. 9. A. B. Cook, *Zeus*, II, 228–9, fig. 159.

12 Imhoof-Blumer, *op. cit.* 203, pl. E. 10. *BMC Pel.* 190 nos. 1–2, pl. 35. 15. B. V. Head, *HN*, 451.

13 F. Brommer, *Vasenlisten²*, 235–6.

14 Jacobsthal, *Die Melischen Reliefs*, no. 27, pl. 15; no. 59, pl. 26; no. 103, pl. 60: note also 185, pl. 70. All are from different moulds.

15 Brommer, *op. cit.* 85–109.

16 *Ol. Forsch.* II (E. Kunze, *Archaische Schildbänder*), 93–102.

17 I suppose that here Phoebe is a by-name for Artemis, cast with pretty irony in the role of mediator. The other girls ought to be Niobe's daughters; there never was a standard nomenclature for the Niobids.

18 Aeschylus perhaps had the nurse and Amphion: for a good summary discussion see Lesky, 649–53.

19 The version that Apollo killed the sons of Niobe when they were out hunting and Artemis killed the daughters in the palace was probably used by Sophocles (see Lesky, 653–4). Lesky also suspects this version in the Niobid painter's krater [3], but the participation of Artemis and a daughter is against him. I doubt if the Niobid painter had thought out his scene so consequentially.

20 *MA* 1906, 289–90, 475, fig. 80. Perhaps second century B.C.

21 Prop. II, 31, 13–14: 'altera deiectos Parnasi vertice Gallos, altera maerebat funera Tantalidos.' The implications are summarised by Lesky, 688: since the Gauls on one half of the doors were in a landscape setting, so too presumably were the Niobids in the other half. The date must have been not later than 28 B.C., when the temple was dedicated; and since the destruction of Gauls at Delphi was not a naturally Roman subject, the carvings were presumably older work, looted from the East though not necessarily Pergamene.

22 Apparently Dinsmoor felt this too, but provided a convenient hillside to give the spectator the necessary vantage point (*AJA* 1939, 39).

23 For some earlier identifications see W. B. Dinsmoor, *AJA* 1939, 38, 40–1; 1943, 20–1. Langlotz's foundlings are:

(1) Berlin, Staatliche Mus. 1958. 1. Torso of wounded male (with hole for arrow). E. Langlotz, *Berliner Mus. Ber.* 1957, 2–5. K. Schefold, *Meisterwerke gr. Kunst*, 76–7, no. 296, fig. on p. 241. G. Hafner, *Ein Apollon-Kopf in Frankfurt*, fig. 12.

(2) Bonn, private collection. Head of female (Artemis?). Langlotz in *Studies presented to D. M. Robinson*, I, 638–47, pls. 63–64 *b*, 65 *a*. Schefold, *op. cit.* no. 297, figs. on p. 239.

(3) Rome, Mus. Cap. 2768. Apollo shooting. Hafner, *op. cit.* figs. 5, 7, 8, 15; he compares very justly a head in Frankfurt. S. Stucchi, *BComm.* LXXV, 3–47, pls. 1–6. Schefold, *op. cit.* no. 294, fig. on p. 241.

24 W. B. Dinsmoor, *AJA* 1939, 27–47. His conclusions are accepted by G. Lippold, *Gr. Plastik*, 201; W.-H. Schuchhardt, *MdI* 1948, 130; W. Fuchs, *AM* 1956, 70 n. 20; E. Lapalus, *Le Fronton sculpté*, 405; and perhaps C. Picard, *MonPiot* XXXIX, 70–2. R. Carpenter (*MAAR* XVIII, 28–9) mentions objections, which he does not feel decisive, of date and material. K. Schefold (*Meisterwerke*, 77) suggests that the three figures came from a pediment of the temple of Ares which was transferred from Acharnae to the Agora of Athens. G. Hafner (*Ein Apollon-Kopf in Frankfurt*, 22–9, 36–7) does not believe that the figures are from a pediment at all. V. Poulsen (*Kunstmuseets Aarsskrift*, 1938, 128) doubts the association of the Terme with the Copenhagen Niobids. No attention is or needs to be given to restorations earlier than Dinsmoor's.

25 The question of date is related to that of school, which also is disputed. The claims of South Italy seem to me best; they have been put most cogently by Hafner, *op. cit.* 43–59.

26 As E. Pfuhl saw (*JdI* 1926, 142 n. 5).

27 See n. 23 (3).

28 Hafner (*op. cit.* 22–9, 36–7) associates the Apollo with the Niobids, but recognises that they would not go together in

a pediment; instead he prefers a free-standing, semicircular group. So freely active a group has no relevant parallels (as far as I know), the figures are not intended to be seen from behind (as the Terme Niobid's left hand makes plain), and anyhow the disparity in size of god and victim remains.

This inaugural lecture was delivered in the University of Cambridge on 1 May 1963

www.ingramcontent.com/pod-product-compliance
Ingram Content Group UK Ltd.
Pitfield, Milton Keynes, MK11 3LW, UK
UKHW042149280225
455719UK00001B/205

9 781107 698468